SECRETS YOU'RE NOT SUPPOSED TO KNOW

THE DARK WEB

The Covert World of Cybercrime

Anita Croy

LUCENT
PRESS

Published in 2019 by
Lucent Press, an Imprint of Greenhaven Publishing, LLC
353 3rd Avenue
Suite 255
New York, NY 10010

For Brown Bear Books Ltd:
Managing Editor: Tim Cooke
Designer: Lynne Lennon
Children's Publisher: Anne O'Daly
Design Manager: Keith Davis
Editorial Director: Lindsey Lowe
Picture Manager: Sophie Mortimer

Picture Credits
t=top, c=center, b=bottom, l=left, r=right
Interior: 123rf: 12; Dreamstime: 4; istockphoto: 34, South Agency 37; Public Domain: 11, Keith Allison, 21,
Dan-Raoul-Miranda, 43, Evan Nesterack, 20; Shutterstock: 7, 17, 1000 words, 24, AGIF, 18, Alice-photo, 25,
Asterick, 23, Alexey Boldin, 19, PT Casimiro, 13, Cineberg, 1, 13, Dragon Images, 10, Drop of Light, 16, drserg,
40, Fotokita, 31, Richard Frazier, 32, Alexander Geiger, 5t, idea Studio, 28, Jeremy Lende, 41, Alexander
Mazurkevich, 27, Sergey Nivens, 8, Wit Olszewski, 36, Unal M. Ozmen, 9, Pe3k, 44, Lizette Potgieter, 33,
Rawpixel.com, 42, Leonard Zhukovsky, 15; US Department of Defense: U.S. Airforce, 26, U.S. Airforce/
Technical Sgt. Cedilio Ricardo, 5cr, U.S. Army/Staff Sgtl Jason Epperson, 45, U.S. Navy/Petty Officer 2md
Class Joshua J. Wahl, 35.
Front cover: Azret Ayubov/Shutterstock

Brown Bear Books has made every attempt to contact the copyright holder.
If anyone has any information please contact licensing@brownbearbooks.co.uk

Cataloging-in-Publication Data

Names: Croy, Anita.
Title: The dark web: the covert world of cybercrime / Anita Croy.
Description: New York : Lucent Press, 2019. | Series: Classified: secrets you're not supposed to know |
Includes glossary and index.
Identifiers: ISBN 9781534564442 (pbk.) | ISBN 9781534564428 (library bound) | ISBN 9781534564435
(ebook)
Subjects: LCSH: Computer crimes--Investigation--Juvenile literature. | Computer crimes--Juvenile literature.
Classification: LCC HV8079.C65 C79 2019 | DDC 364.16'8--dc23

Manufactured in the United States of America

CPSIA Compliance Information: Batch #BS18KL
For further information contact Rosen Publishing, New York, New York at 1-800-237-9932

CONTENTS

COMPUTER CRIMES

Most people would say that the rise of the Internet has been positive. It makes everyday tasks more convenient and makes it easier to access information.

Not everything connected with the Internet has been a benefit, however. Almost as soon as Internet use became common in the 1990s, criminals saw it as an opportunity to expand their illegal operations. The more people went online to do their shopping or banking, for example, the more criminals tried to steal enough information to impersonate them. Meanwhile, **extremists** and terrorists used the World Wide Web to circulate messages of hatred and violence around the world.

>> Hacked Some criminals freeze people's computers until a sum of money, called a ransom, is paid.

>> **Identity** Criminals employ skilled computer scientists who can access people's online information to steal their identity.

IN THE DARK

Criminal and extremist activity come together in a hidden part of the web called the Dark Web. This is a place where no users can be traced and data is **encrypted**. That encourages illegal activity such as buying and selling drugs. The existence of the Dark Web attracts criticism. Those who defend the freedom of the Internet claim that the Dark Web can be a force for good—but they face a tough time convincing others of their argument.

>> **Cyber War**
The U.S. Army has its own command to defend the country from hostile attacks.

IDENTITY THEFT

Many Internet transactions require users to prove who they are. Users do this with personal details, but that makes those details open to being stolen.

B eing online brings risks. Almost anything that involves a financial transaction online requires users to input personal information. This could be just an email address but is more likely to include information such as an address, date of birth, or even the name of a favorite pet. For criminals, this kind of personal information is valuable. If they can get access to the details, they can use them to steal your online identity. They can then pretend to be you in order to steal your money.

In 2012, it was estimated that 16.6 million Americans had been the victims of identity **fraud**. That is 7 percent of all U.S. residents over age 16. In the United Kingdom, meanwhile, more than four out of every five cases of identity fraud are now committed online. This online identity theft is a relatively new crime. It is highly profitable for criminals. It is also a constant challenge for people fighting online fraud.

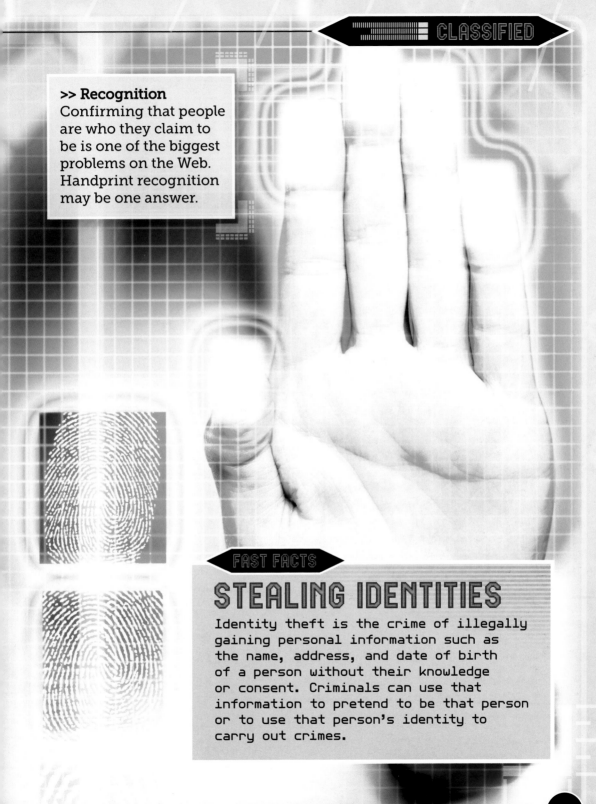

>> Recognition

Confirming that people are who they claim to be is one of the biggest problems on the Web. Handprint recognition may be one answer.

FAST FACTS

STEALING IDENTITIES

Identity theft is the crime of illegally gaining personal information such as the name, address, and date of birth of a person without their knowledge or consent. Criminals can use that information to pretend to be that person or to use that person's identity to carry out crimes.

INCREASED SECURITY

PINs and passwords are notoriously easy for determined **hackers** to figure out. Computer experts plan to use advanced technology to create passwords based on a person's unique **biometric** data. They want to use iris recognition or fingerprints to create a password impossible for hackers to copy or steal. However, criminals are already working on a way to **replicate** irises. Perhaps even the new technology will not be foolproof.

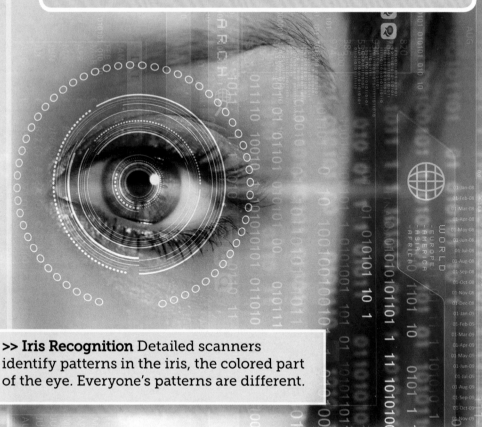

>> Iris Recognition Detailed scanners identify patterns in the iris, the colored part of the eye. Everyone's patterns are different.

Before the rise of the Internet, criminals who wanted to pretend to be someone else had to get their hands dirty. One way of stealing a person's identity was known as dumpster diving. It involved sifting through the contents of old paper in trash cans. Criminals were trying to find names, addresses, and any other personal information that would enable them to impersonate someone else.

>> **Wallet** In the past, identity theft required criminals to get hold of documents or cards.

ID THEFT IN HISTORY

In the 19th century, many cases of identity theft in the United States were related to elections. Political parties encouraged their supporters to steal voter registration cards or use other fake ID to vote more than once in elections. The next wave of identity fraud came in the 1930s, when liquor became legal at the end of **Prohibition**. Each state could set its own legal drinking age, so young people crossed state lines to drink in states with lower age limits. In most cases, they needed ID to prove their age. Fake IDs soon became big business. Fake IDs continued to be popular after 1984, when Congress passed a federal law setting the national legal drinking age at 21.

>> **Record** Magnetic strips on bank cards can give criminals access to large stores of data.

Another wave of identity fraud was connected to immigration. In 1986, Congress passed a law requiring employers to prove that all their employees were entitled to work legally. Potential employees needed to show potential employers a social security number and driver's license. Some illegal immigrants used stolen social security numbers to create fake ID documents.

THAT'S ME!

The term "identity" fraud was first used in 1964. In the modern form of the crime, experts distinguish between two main types of identity fraud. The first is true-name identity theft. In this fraud, the criminal takes an individual's personal information and uses it to open a new bank account.

Once they have done that, it is easy to take out a cell-phone contract or a checking account in the account holder's name, which the account holder is paying for. The other type of identity fraud is known as account-takeover identity theft. In this fraud, a criminal uses an individual's personal information to gain access to their existing accounts. They change the mailing address on the victim's bank and credit card accounts. They can run up huge bills before the victim realizes what has happened.

>> **Belgium** All Belgians over age 12 must carry an ID card with them at all times.

WHAT DO YOU THINK?

Identity fraud is not as common in continental Europe as it is in the United States and in Great Britain. Experts think this may be because virtually everyone across Europe carries a photo ID card. In Belgium, for example, citizens have to carry their ID cards at all times. Do you think ID cards might cut identity theft in the United States? If so, would you be happy to carry an ID card, as everyone does in Belgium?

The Internet has made both these types of identity fraud easier, because transactions require no personal interaction. Stealing a person's bank details before the Internet was more difficult. It would have involved visiting a bank and pretending to be the victim. There was a high chance of being caught.

HOW IS IT DONE?

Today, criminals use a range of methods to carry out ID theft. There are even apps to help them. Phishing is a common and very successful means of online stealing. Criminals send emails that seem to be from a target's bank or another financial institution such as the Inland Revenue Service (IRS).

FOR AND AGAINST

All banks warn their customers not to reveal their passwords. However, customers sometimes receive emails claiming to be from their bank that link to what looks like the bank's website. When asked, they enter their password, and criminals then empty their account. Some people think such theft is the customer's responsibility for ignoring the bank's instructions. Others argue that the bank has a duty to spot fraudulent activity on any account.

>> **Bank Cards** Do users have a responsibility for protecting the details of their own accounts?

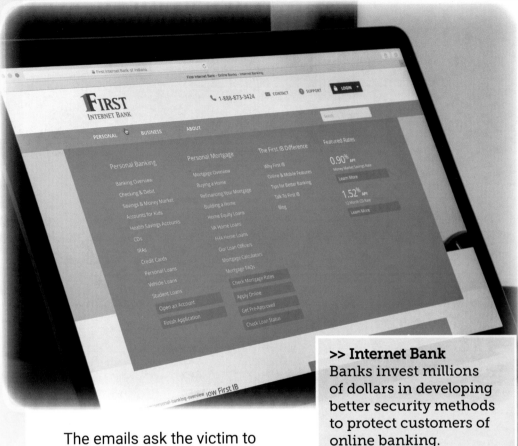

> **>> Internet Bank**
> Banks invest millions of dollars in developing better security methods to protect customers of online banking.

The emails ask the victim to supply their bank account details or to click on a link. Both of these allow the criminal to access the user's bank details and steal their money. In a similar fraud, criminals set up fake accounts on selling websites. Users enter their information to purchase goods that never arrive. Meanwhile, the criminals have their details. Another way to steal personal information is by infecting the victim's computer with a **virus**. The virus allows criminals to invade the computer from a remote location and steal any personal data stored on it.

EXTREMISM AND TERRORISM

The attacks of 9/11 in 2001 were a new form of terrorism. Since then, the growth of the Internet has coincided with the rise of both extremism and terrorism.

Since 2001, the threat of worldwide terrorism has expanded. One of its sources comes from groups that follow an extreme form of Islam. Wars in Afghanistan and Iraq, and a civil war in Syria, created a breeding ground for such groups. One of these groups is called the Islamic State group, also known in English as Islamic State of Iraq and Syria (ISIS) or in Arabic as Daesh. ISIS recruits people with computer and marketing skills to give it a high online profile. It uses both social media and the Dark Web to spread **propaganda** and recruit new members. It encourages young Muslims in other countries to become **radicalized**. Some of these young people have gone on to carry out terrorist attacks. The Internet has become a platform for extreme opinions. The question of whether extremists should be allowed uncensored access to the public via the Internet is one of the most pressing issues of the modern age.

>> **Attack** An FBI notice seeks information after a terrorist attack in New York City in October 2017.

FOR INFORMATION

The FBI and NYPD are seeking the public's assistance in the investigation into the terrorist act that occurred in Lower Manhattan earlier today. The public is urged to share any images or videos that could assist in the investigation to the FBI link: www.fbi.gov/nyctribeca.

In addition, any information to a
can
FBI
the
Hotl
Spa

CALL: 1-800-577-8477 (TIPS)

FAST FACTS

NETWORK OF TERROR

Radical Islamist groups use the Internet to promote their own interpretation of Islam, which is rejected by almost all other Muslims. These groups set out to radicalize new recruits in the hopes that they will carry out terrorist attacks in their own countries.

>> **Shrine** Parisians light candles in memory of those who died in the 2015 attacks on the city.

ORGANIZING TERRORISM

On November 13, 2015, terrorists launched coordinated attacks in the French capital, Paris. They attacked an international soccer match, a rock concert venue, and bars and restaurants. The attacks killed 130 people and left hundreds more injured. The attacks were organized online. The terrorists used encrypted digital communications to plan their actions. Despite this sophisticated planning, one of the gunmen made an error. He tossed his cell phone into a trash can. When police recovered the phone, they used its **location services** to trace a terrorist hideout. Police raided the hideout, killing two terrorists and arresting eight more.

THE PROPAGANDA WAR

The Internet is a worldwide platform for extremists and terrorists. In the past, people traditionally aired their views by writing to newspapers or even by standing in the street to address members of the public. Their audiences were small. In addition, newspaper editors or passersby could challenge facts that were not true. Today, anyone with access to a cell phone can reach millions of people by posting on the Internet. The people looking at the posts have no context to be able to tell whether something is true or not. Like others involved in terrorist attacks, the Paris attackers had watched online material posted by ISIS. They allied themselves to the group.

FOR AND AGAINST

In March 2017, a terrorist named Khalid Masood drove a car into pedestrians on Westminster Bridge in London, U.K. Five people died as a result of the attack. Masood was shot dead. Police discovered that Masood used WhatsApp to send an encrypted message just before the attack. WhatsApp refused to reveal the contents of the message. It said its users had to be confident that it would protect their anonymity. The police argue that social media organizations should have a legal obligation to reveal such information.

>> **Westminster Bridge**
A policeman adds flowers to tributes left after the attack.

>> Soccer World Cup
In 2014, the terrorist group ISIS hijacked the hashtag #worldcup to broadcast violent and barbaric propaganda.

Sometimes, people who claim to act in the name of ISIS have had no direct contact with the organization. In fall 2017, for example, a terrorist used a rental truck to kill eight people in Manhattan. The suspect was an immigrant to the United States from Uzbekistan named Sayfullo Saipov. He claimed allegiance to ISIS after watching its online propaganda.

ISIS not only releases propaganda videos; it also encourages its members to tweet and to post images on Instagram. Often these images are of extreme brutality. ISIS uses hashtags to make sure its messages are widely shared while their creators remain hidden on the Dark Web.

SOCIAL MEDIA

Facebook and Twitter may help terrorists and criminals, but they are also helping the police. Police not only monitor online communications. They also interact with criminals to gather evidence. In Brooklyn, one officer befriended a member of a gang and followed his bragging on social media about the gang's crimes. When the gang discussed an upcoming burglary, the police followed them and caught them in the act.

TOP SECRET

>> **Social sharing** Many people like to broadcast their activity on social media.

WHAT DO YOU THINK?

Within the United States there are extremist groups with a wide range of beliefs. The Alt-Right, or Alternative Right, includes a number of right-wing groups. They include white supremacists, who believe white people are superior to other races. In August 2017, white supremacists clashed with left-wing demonstrators from the Alt-Left in a rally at Charlottesville, Virginia. One protestor against the rally died. President Trump reacted by suggesting that left-wing extremists are just as bad as right-wing extremists. Do you agree?

>> **White Supremacy**
Right-wing marchers fight police at a rally in Charlottesville in August 2017.

CYBERTERRORISM

As well as changing the nature of traditional terrorism, the Internet has also enabled the rise of cyberterrorism. Cyberterrorism is the use of computers to launch organized, carefully planned, online attacks against both ordinary people and government **infrastructure**. Cyberterrorism did not really exist before 2011, because the technology it requires was not sophisticated enough. By 2013, U.S. intelligence agencies rated it the number one threat facing the country.

Cyberterrorism attacks struck Estonia in 2007, South Korea in 2013, and Ukraine in 2017. The attacks disabled banks, phone networks, and electricity supplies. The attacks on Estonia and Ukraine likely came from Russia, which had disputes with those countries at the time. The attack on South Korea probably came from North Korea.

U.S. intelligence said that Russia was also responsible for spreading misinformation during the U.S. presidential election of 2016. In the debate in fall 2017 about whether NFL players should kneel during the national anthem, Russian **bot** accounts flooded both sides of the argument, sending tweets using the hashtags #Takeaknee and #BoycottNFL, ensuring that the number of tweets enflamed the debate further.

>> **Taking the Knee** Russian bots filled Twitter with tweets on both sides of the dispute involving NFL players in fall 2017.

CYBER WARFARE

Wars are no longer fought only with bullets and bombs, but with computers. Cyber warfare has been around for a few decades, but it has become more common in the last 10 years.

In the United States, a cyberattack is classified as an act of war. Cyber warfare uses computer technology to disrupt the normal functioning of enemy states. This might take the form of hacking energy companies to disrupt supplies, freezing the accounting systems of banks, or stealing the personal information of millions of citizens. Cyber warfare takes advantage of the fact that virtually all areas of military, political, and economic activity now depend on computers.

Cyber warfare has a number of advantages over **conventional warfare**. One is that it is less costly in terms of lives. Another is that conventional warfare, which uses bombs and other weapons, destroys any enemy infrastructure that is attacked. Cyber warfare merely disables systems temporarily. They can easily be reinstated at a later date.

>> North Korea

North Korea's army has a small geographical reach—but cyber warfare carries its influence around the globe.

WAR GAMES

Today's governments and large corporations are frequently involved in war games. These are strategic cybersecurity exercises designed to test a computer system's ability to withstand a cyberattack. Penetration tests aim to copy the techniques used by real attackers in order to expose weaknesses within a system and to test how people respond when they are under attack.

WHO DID IT?

Most nations are reluctant to admit being involved in cyber warfare. For example, U.S. officials believe China was behind a hack of the U.S. Office of Personnel Management in 2014, but China did not confirm its involvement. The United States also believes Iran was behind an attack on the control system of a dam in New York State in 2013, but the Iranians have said nothing about it. In contrast, the **rogue** state of North Korea made no efforts to disguise their use of cyber warfare. In 2014, Sony Pictures released a movie called *The Interview*. The comedy made fun of North Korea.

>> **The Interview** In Sony's 2014 comedy, U.S. journalists accidentally **assassinate** the leader of North Korea, Kim Jong-un.

FOR AND AGAINST

In 2017, hackers launched a cyberattack on the U.K. Houses of Parliament in London. They used stolen security data to access the email accounts of members of the House of Commons and House of Lords, as well as advisers and staff. The attack was detected after about 90 accounts had been hacked. Access to the computer system was shut down for anyone not physically inside the Houses of Parliament. Security experts were certain they had stopped a full-scale attack developing. They believed the attack was backed by a hostile government. The likely sources of the attack were either Iran or North Korea.

>> **Houses of Parliament** The U.K parliament computer system came under attack.

Soon afterward, the Sony Pictures computer network was hacked by a group called the Guardians of Peace. Thousands of emails, social security numbers, and even unreleased movies were leaked. The entertainment company lost half of its data.

The U.S. government concluded that North Korea was behind the attack. It imposed **sanctions** on North Korea. A month later, the North Korean Internet was shut down for 10 hours. That might have been an example of U.S. cyber warfare—but the government has not commented one way or the other.

CYBER COMMAND

To fight cyber warfare, the U.S. Army created Cyber Command, which became fully operational in September 2017. Cyber Command, or the 780th Military Intelligence Brigade, aims to stop attacks from enemies while keeping open domestic computer networks. Its mission statement states, "Cyberspace operations are critical to our nation and the Army's mission. Securing cyberspace is a 24/7 responsibility."

>> **Lviv** The Ukrainian capital was left without power on a bitterly cold winter's day.

WINTER ATTACK

During the winter of 2015, a quarter of a million people in eastern Ukraine suffered a sudden power outage. The power remained off for up to six hours as the thermometer plunged to 0°F (−18°C). The Ukrainians quickly blamed the Russians for an act of cyber warfare. Investigations revealed that Black Energy **malware** from Russia had carried out an attack.

To make things more confusing, the cyberattack probably did not cause the power outage. However, the malware did allow the hackers to get into the computer systems that controlled electricity generating plants. Power was only restored when workers switched their systems to manual.

The cyberattacks on Ukraine were part of a larger campaign by Russia. Not only did Russian groups carry out 6,500 cyberattacks on 36 Ukrainian targets in two months, Russian troops also invaded eastern Ukraine. Russia claims parts of Ukrainian territory. Many Russians living in Ukraine wish to become part of Russia. The cyberattacks were part of a hostile campaign to weaken Ukraine's government.

CAN CYBER WARFARE BE STOPPED?

Stopping hackers is not easy. If hackers are caught, they can only be sent for trial if there is an **extradition** treaty between the country where they are based and the country they attacked. Even the existence of a treaty does not mean a trial will take place. In 2001 and 2002, a Scottish computer scientist named Gary McKinnon hacked into computer systems belonging to the U.S. military and to NASA.

WHAT DO YOU THINK?

Security experts try to figure out the best protection from cyberattack. One problem they face is that, because computer programs are written by humans, most programs have weaknesses that can be exploited. It may be that computer technology advances so fast that computers can write complex codes for other computers. Will any computer system ever be 100 percent safe?

McKinnon claimed that he was looking for hidden evidence of UFO activity. The U.S. military said McKinnon disrupted computers, supplies, and other key systems. The United States requested McKinnon's extradition from the United Kingdom. After a long legal process, the British government halted extradition in 2012. It argued that McKinnon suffered from depression and might harm himself if he were sent for trial. The United States continued to regard McKinnon as a cyberterrorist—but had no means to try or punish him.

>> Cyber Experts
The U.S. Army hires some of the smartest computer scientists in the country to help prevent cyberattacks.

THE DARK WEB

The Internet is like an iceberg. The most popular sites on the World Wide Web are above water, but most of the Internet is hidden from view. Part of this hidden region is known as the Dark Web.

The Dark Web is the most sinister part of the Internet. It is relatively difficult to access—and impossible to access by chance. Unlike the normal web, where it is possible to trace users' identities on search engines and websites, on the Dark Web users are completely anonymous. The Dark Web has become the location of much illegal activity. Criminals use it to buy and sell illegal goods such as guns and drugs. Terrorists use it to pass on messages about planned attacks.

Not everyone views the Dark Web as wholly negative. Some people see it as a safe space for human rights and political activists, **whistleblowers**, and journalists to work. Such commentators can use the Dark Web to reveal corrupt practices without revealing their identity. Whistleblowers such as the WikiLeaks website use the privacy tools of the Dark Web to release confidential data. In 2013, U.S. intelligence contractor Edward Snowden used the Dark Web to release thousands of classified documents from the National Security Agency (NSA) to journalists. Releasing such material is illegal, but Snowden believed it was for the public good.

>> **Anonymous** On the Dark Web, neither people who create websites or people who visit the sites can be identified.

FAST FACTS

NET STRUCTURE

About 90 percent of the Internet is not accessible by normal browsers. The largest part of this is the Deep Web. It is a virtual store for excess or old webpages. The Dark Web is part of the Web that can only be accessed using special software that keeps its users anonymous. It is home to hidden chatrooms and even its own Wiki-type guides on finding your way around.

The documents revealed secret practices by intelligence agencies, such as the widespread **surveillance** of U.S. citizens. Snowden revealed that the NSA read the emails of millions of Americans and that major Internet companies helped it do so. Verizon helped it log the time and location of phone calls—though not their content. The revelations caused a storm. German chancellor Angela Merkel complained that the NSA had spied on her emails. Snowden fled to Russia to avoid arrest. The NSA was forced to defend its policy by claiming that it was trying to find evidence to prevent future terrorist attacks. Civil liberties groups complained that this did not justify its lack of regard for the privacy of U.S. citizens.

>> **Leaks** The Dark Web is a source of leaks. Supporters claim these leaks help to prevent secrecy in politics.

>> Afghanistan
The Dark Web can give a voice to people who might otherwise be silenced.

ESCAPING GOVERNMENT CONTROL

In countries such as China and Iran, governments control the media, including the Internet. The Dark Web gives users a way to publish material the government would prevent them from releasing. For example, a young woman in a country such as Afghanistan, where women's freedoms are restricted, might use the Dark Web to blog while remaining anonymous.

FOR AND AGAINST

In 2010, WikiLeaks released classified details of U.S. military operations in Afghanistan and Iraq. The United States wanted to try the founder of WikiLeaks, Julian Assange. He claimed asylum from Ecuador in 2012 and began living in its embassy in London. Assange's supporters say he stands for transparent government and free speech. The U.S. government argues that he is a criminal whose leaks endangered U.S. military personnel.

https://www.torproject.org

Ho

Anonymity Online
Protect your privacy. Defend yourself against network surveillance and traffic analysis.

>> **Browser** The Tor browser routes communications via thousands of computers, so they are almost impossible to follow.

HIDING YOUR IDENTITY

The Dark Web is a recruiting ground for terrorists, who can avoid detection. Terrorist and extremist organizations use the Dark Web to communicate with supporters without being traced. This makes it easier for terrorists to work with recruits in other countries.

Criminals and terrorists on the Dark Web use the Tor browser to hide their identities. Tor also hides the sites being looked at and allows users to disguise their physical location. Every computer has a unique Internet Protocol (IP) address that enables its activity to be traced. On the Dark Web, users have Virtual Private Networks (VPNs) to hide their IP addresses. They add operating systems that alert them if their online activity is being tracked. For additional security, users communicate using an encrypted email server.

WHAT DO YOU THINK?

In June 2017, the U.S. Department of Justice seized and shut down AlphaBay. The site was one of the biggest marketplaces on the Dark Web for illegal drugs. It had 40,000 vendors and more than 200,000 users. At the same time, Dutch authorities shut down Hansa, a similar site. The owners of the sites were arrested and their **assets** were seized. The Department of Justice said the actions showed that the Dark Web did not offer the levels of anonymity criminals thought it did. Do you think such high-profile actions might make criminals think twice about operating on the Dark Web?

THIS HIDDEN SITE HAS BEEN SEIZED

Since July 4, 2017

as a part of a law enforcement operation by the Federal Bureau of Investigation, the Drug Enforcement Administration, and European law enforcement agencies acting through Europol.

In accordance with the law of European Union member states and obtained pursuant to a forfeiture order by the United States Attorney's Office for the Eastern District of California and the U.S. Department of Justice's Computer Crime & Intellectual Property Section.

This seizure was part of **Operation Bayonet**, which includes the takeover of Hansa Market by the National Police of the Netherlands on June 20, 2017, and the takedown of AlphaBay Market by the Federal Bureau of Investigation of the United States of America on July 4, 2017.

HANSA   AlphaBay Market

POLITIE   EUROPOL   NCA

Such servers send encrypted emails as **spam** that passes between hundreds of email accounts. Only the intended recipient has the code needed to read the message. Even if the recipient's account is being monitored by security forces, this technique makes it impossible to tell who sent the original message.

NEW MONEY

The Dark Web has become a global marketplace for illegal goods and services. This is because it does not operate with ordinary currencies. Instead, users of the Dark Web use so-called **cryptocurrencies** to transfer funds.

BITCOIN

The cryptocurrency **bitcoin** was invented by an unknown person or people known as Satoshi Nakamoto. He disappeared in 2010, having first set a limit on the total of bitcoins that could exist as 21 million. This limit helps define the value of the currency. Anyone can download a bitcoin wallet and buy bitcoins through a currency exchange. Although bitcoins are often used for illegal activity, buying and selling them is not illegal.

>> Bitcoin
This illustration of a bitcoin is just that—no physical bitcoins exist.

>> **Payment** Cryptocurrencies are untraceable, so they have made it easier to carry out illegal trade without fear of being caught.

The best known of these currencies is bitcoin, which became the first digital currency when it was introduced in 2009. Bitcoin has no independent value—only the value its users give it. It has grown rapidly in popularity. In 2015, there were 100,000 bitcoin transactions that took place every day. That number continues to grow.

Given that many people on the Dark Web are criminals, how can they be trusted to pay one another? The system relies on a process known as escrow, in which cryptocurrency is paid to a third party. The third party holds on to it until a transaction has taken place. The system works well, even though it relies on both the seller and the buyer putting their faith in the third party—and the criminals of the Dark Web!

WHO RUNS THE WEB?

The World Wide Web was intended to be free and unregulated. In many ways, it seems that it is. But who really controls how everyone uses the Web?

In 1989, the British scientist Tim Berners-Lee was working as a software engineer at the European Organization for Nuclear Research (CERN) in Switzerland when he had the idea of allowing individual computers to share information. As Berners-Lee developed his idea (the World Wide Web) it became clear that it would only reach its potential if it remained free to use and unrestricted by **regulations**.

Almost 30 years later, the Web has transformed beyond anything Berners-Lee imagined, but it continues to be free to use. In theory, it is also unrestricted by regulations. However, even though no one apparently "runs" the Internet, many organizations and individuals have an influence on the Web and how we use it. Some people argue that, although it may appear that the Web is a free space, it is effectively controlled by powerful groups whose identity is not always clear.

>> **Guy Fawkes Mask** The hackers' group Anonymous claims to fight for freedom from regulation on the Internet. Members are known for wearing masks like this one in public.

FAST FACTS

DOMAIN NAMES

One way of controlling the web is through controlling the domain name system (DNS). This series of registers links web addresses to IP addresses, which are long lists of numbers. Without domain names, users would have to remember long sequences of numbers for every site they visited. Domain names are regulated by the Internet Corporation for Assigned Names and Numbers (ICANN).

SOURCES OF INFLUENCE

Many different organizations shape the Web. They include companies who build **hardware** to access the Web, such as Apple, or companies that build servers. They also include Internet service providers (ISPs), such as Verizon or Virgin Media. Large online retailers such as Amazon and eBay also influence users' behavior. Internet corporations such as Google and Facebook are also highly influential. In 2017, 26 percent of U.S. adults got all their news from social media, mainly from Facebook. Facebook sends personalized news stories to users based on their profile, so people only see stories they are likely to like. Facebook has admitted that some past stories have been biased.

WHAT DO YOU THINK?

When Sir Tim Berners-Lee (right) invented the World Wide Web, he knew that it had great potential. However, no one realized just how powerful it would become. Knowing what we now know, what would you change if we started the Web today? Would you put in more controls or less anonymity? Or perhaps more protection from goverment interference or rules against spreading fake news?

>> **Google** An online search engine such as Google helps direct users by ranking sites in a particular order.

IN THE BACKGROUND

A series of less well-known organizations are responsible for the structure and maintenance of the Internet. Some **conspiracy theorists** accuse them of having too much power over the Internet. These organizations include ICANN (see page 39), which distributes domain names, and the International Telecommunication Union (ITU), which resolves disputes between nations about the Internet. The Internet Architecture Board (IAB) is responsible for the Internet's technical development. The Internet Society (ISOC) tries to ensure that the Internet is fair and up to date. The Internet Engineering Task Force (IETF) is a voluntary group. It provides high-quality information to engineers who want to help develop parts of the Internet.

CONTROLLING ACCESS

Many Web users across the world do not have the luxury of choosing which sites to look at. They live in countries where the Internet is **censored** by their governments to silence political opposition. In North Korea, all websites are under government control, but only around 4 percent of the population have Internet access, anyway. Around 400,000 sites have been blocked in Saudi Arabia. They include any that mention political, social, or religious topics that do not fit the Islamic beliefs of the royal family. In Iran, all bloggers are required to register with the Ministry of Art and Culture. If they blog without permission or write negative comments about the regime, bloggers can be jailed.

>> **Iran** Bloggers in Iran face imprisonment for a range of "crimes" against the country.

The country with the strictest Internet control is China. It blocks every site that contains information it does not like and it also erases content. For example, Chinese websites cannot mention the failed democracy movement in Tiananmen Square in 1989.

BLOGGER IN JAIL

Raif Badawi is a blogger from Saudi Arabia. His posts differed from the conservative view of Islam followed by the country's rulers. In 2012, he was put on trial in Saudi Arabia. Badawi was found guilty of insulting Islam through electronic channels. He was sentenced to seven years in prison and 600 lashes. The sentence was later increased. Badawi received the first 50 lashes in January 2015. His wife, Ensaf Haidar, fled to Canada after her husband's trial. She says he is not physically strong enough to survive further punishment.

TOP SECRET

>> **Norway** Protests were held around the world to object to the lashing of Raif Badawi.

FOR AND AGAINST

Facebook has a global reach and more than 1 billion active users. In contrast, the U.S. government governs only about 325 million Americans. Some people say this means Internet corporations such as Facebook have become more powerful than governments. Others say it is impossible to compare a commercial organization with a government that has the power to make laws. However, those who believe Facebook has more power suggest that the part played by Facebook posts in the 2016 U.S. presidential election, which might have swayed the result, proves their point.

 ← → C ⌂ 🔒 Secure | https://www.facebook.com/DonaldTrump/

f Donald J. Trump 🔍

Donald J. Trump ✔
@DonaldTrump

>> **Facebook Page**
U.S. president Donald Trump makes his opinions known by Facebook and Twitter.

>> **Leaked** In 2010 WikiLeaks released millions of classified documents about U.S. military action in Afghanistan and Iraq.

It is not only governments who seek to control the Internet. When WikiLeaks released classified U.S. military documents in 2010, Visa blocked WikiLeaks' access to its financial accounts and Amazon stopped hosting WikiLeaks on its servers. In return, Hackers Anonymous crashed the websites of Visa, Amazon, and other companies that took measures against WikiLeaks. Both sides of the dispute denied the other access to the Web—at least for a short time.

THE CHANGING WEB

In today's world, access to the Web is widely seen as a basic requirement. However, the evolving Web faces many challenges, such as cybercrime, extremism, criminal activity, and the spread of false news stories. Many people believe that it is in the interests of all its users that such challenges are overcome as soon as possible.

GLOSSARY

assassinate To murder someone for a political reason.

assets Items of property owned by an individual or company.

biometric Relating to the statistical analysis of biological information.

bitcoin A unit of an online currency.

bot A computer program that automatically searches for information on the Internet.

censored Having communications limited by authorities.

conspiracy theorists People who believe that secret but powerful organizations are responsible for unexplained events.

conventional warfare Wars fought with physical weapons, such as guns.

cryptocurrencies Currencies that only exist in a virtual form online.

encrypted Converted into a code.

extradition Handing a wanted person from one country to another for trial.

extremists People who believe in strict, extreme forms of religion or politics.

fraud Deception for financial gain.

hackers Criminals who access computer systems without authority.

hardware Physical equipment, such as computers, cables, and servers.

infrastructure The basic physical structures and networks a society needs to function, such as roads.

location services Apps on a cell phone that use satellites to figure out its geographical location.

malware Software designed to damage or gain access to other computers.

PINs Personal identification numbers, used to access ATMs.

Prohibition The period from 1920 to 1933 when selling alcohol was forbidden in the United States.

propaganda Material designed to get people to support or oppose a particular point of view.

radicalized Encouraged to adopt extreme positions about social or religious issues.

regulations Rules of behavior.

replicate To make an exact copy of something.

rogue Behaving in ways that are dangerous or not normal, such as a country not following international laws.

sanctions Penalties imposed for breaking the law.

spam Uninvited emails sent to large numbers of computer users.

surveillance The close observation of people.

virus A piece of computer code that reproduces itself, destroying data.

whistleblowers People who reveal unlawful or immoral activity.

FURTHER RESOURCES

Books

Anniss, Matt. *Cyber Wars*. New York, NY: Cavendish Square Publishing, 2018.

Gitlin, Martin, and Margaret J. Goldstein. *Cyber Attack*. Minneapolis, MN: Twenty-First Century Books, 2015.

Harmon, Daniel E. *Cyber Attacks, Counterattacks, and Espionage*. New York, NY: Rosen Publishing, 2017.

Stewart, Melissa. *Tim Berners-Lee, Inventor of the World Wide Web*. New York, NY: Chelsea House, 2013.

Websites

How Hackers Work
computer.howstuffworks.com/hacker.htm
How Stuff Works explains how computer hackers operate.

How Identity Theft Works
money.howstuffworks.com/identity-theft.htm
This article from How Stuff Works explains how criminals steal identities and use them.

US Army Cyber Command
www.arcyber.army.mil
Check out the home page of the U.S. Army Cyber Command.

INDEX

DATE DUE

PRINTED IN U.S.A.